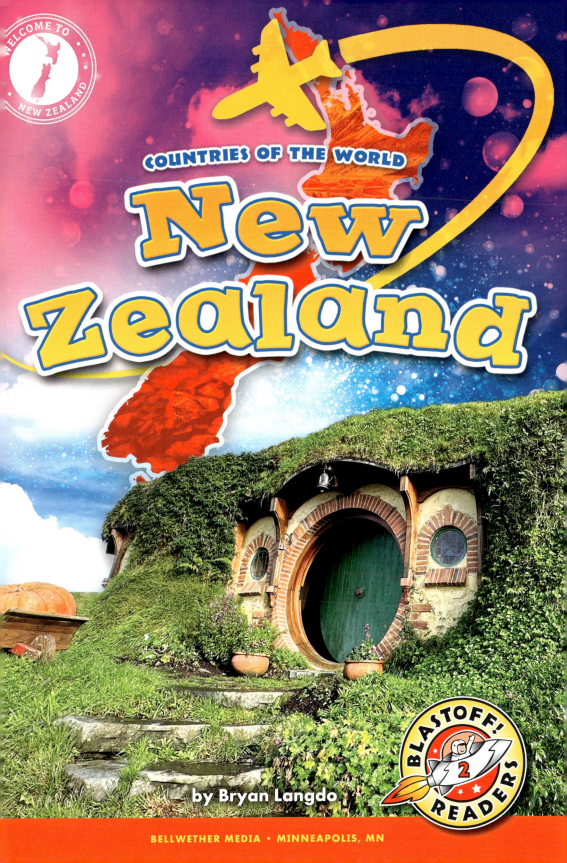

Blastoff! Readers are carefully developed by literacy experts to build reading stamina and move students toward fluency by combining standards-based content with developmentally appropriate text.

 Level 1 provides the most support through repetition of high-frequency words, light text, predictable sentence patterns, and strong visual support.

 Level 2 offers early readers a bit more challenge through varied sentences, increased text load, and text-supportive special features.

 Level 3 advances early-fluent readers toward fluency through increased text load, less reliance on photos, advancing concepts, longer sentences, and more complex special features.

★ **Blastoff! Universe**

 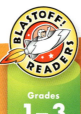 

Reading Level — Grade K → Grades 1–3 → Grade 4

This edition first published in 2026 by Bellwether Media, Inc.

No part of this publication may be reproduced in whole or in part without written permission of the publisher. For information regarding permission, write to Bellwether Media, Inc., Attention: Permissions Department, 3500 American Blvd W, Suite 150, Bloomington, MN 55431.

Library of Congress Cataloging-in-Publication Data

LC record for New Zealand available at: https://lccn.loc.gov/2025015022

Text copyright © 2026 by Bellwether Media, Inc. BLASTOFF! READERS and associated logos are trademarks and/or registered trademarks of Bellwether Media, Inc. Bellwether Media is a division of FlutterBee Education Group.

Editor: Betsy Rathburn   Designer: Laura Sowers

Printed in the United States of America, North Mankato, MN.

Table of Contents

All About New Zealand	4
Land and Animals	6
Life in New Zealand	12
New Zealand Facts	20
Glossary	22
To Learn More	23
Index	24

All About New Zealand

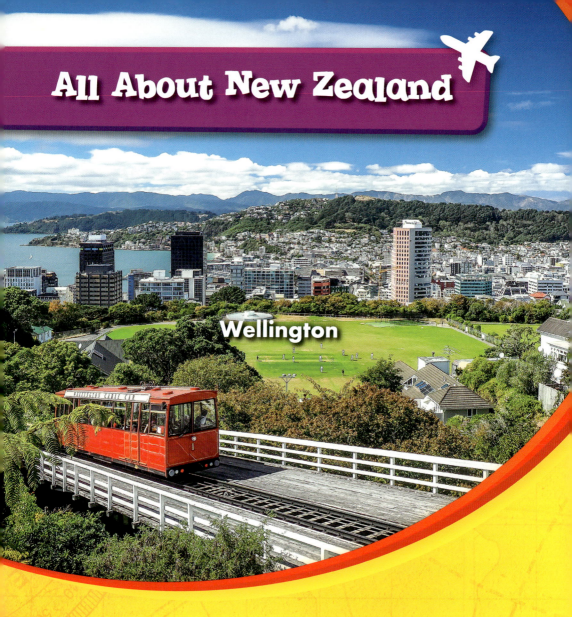

Wellington

New Zealand is a country in the South Pacific Ocean. Its capital is Wellington.

The country is home to kiwi birds. New Zealanders are often called Kiwis!

Land and Animals

New Zealand has two main islands. The North Island has many **hot springs** and **volcanoes**.

The South Island has tall mountains. The biggest are in the Southern Alps.

hot spring

Aoraki

Size: 12,316 feet (3,754 meters) tall
Famous For: New Zealand's highest mountain, also known as Mount Cook

New Zealand has a mild **climate**.

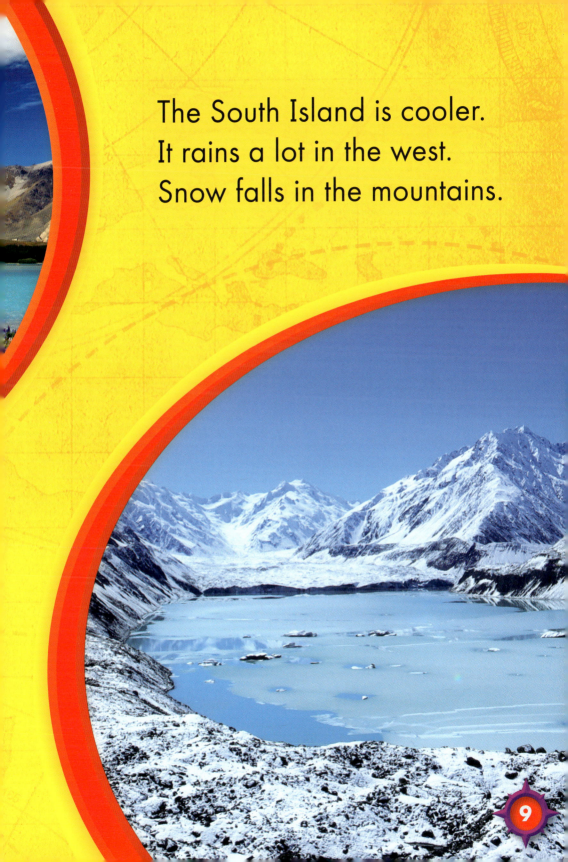

The South Island is cooler.
It rains a lot in the west.
Snow falls in the mountains.

Kiwis catch worms in forests.
Keas fly in the mountains.
Tuataras hunt **insects**.

kea

Animals of New Zealand

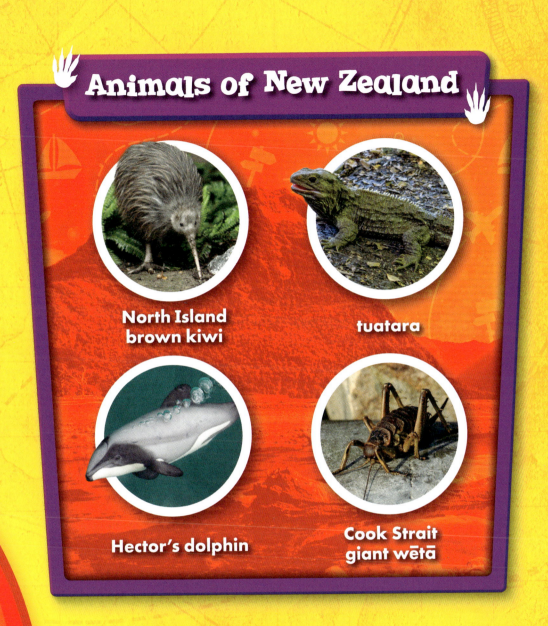

North Island brown kiwi

tuatara

Hector's dolphin

Cook Strait giant wētā

Dolphins swim off the coasts. Wētās creep on the South Island at night!

Life in New Zealand

Most New Zealanders have a European **background**. The Māori are an **Indigenous** group. People speak English or Māori.

Most people live in cities. The biggest city is Auckland.

Auckland

traditional Māori performance

The arts are important in New Zealand. Māori people perform **traditional** songs.

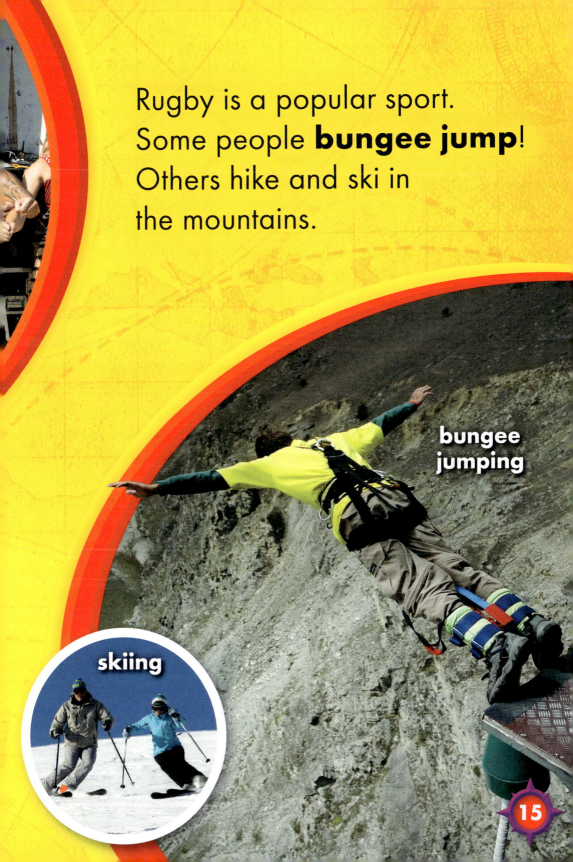

Rugby is a popular sport. Some people **bungee jump**! Others hike and ski in the mountains.

bungee jumping

skiing

Fish and chips is a favorite food. Meat pies are popular, too. *Rēwena* is Māori bread.

New Zealand Foods

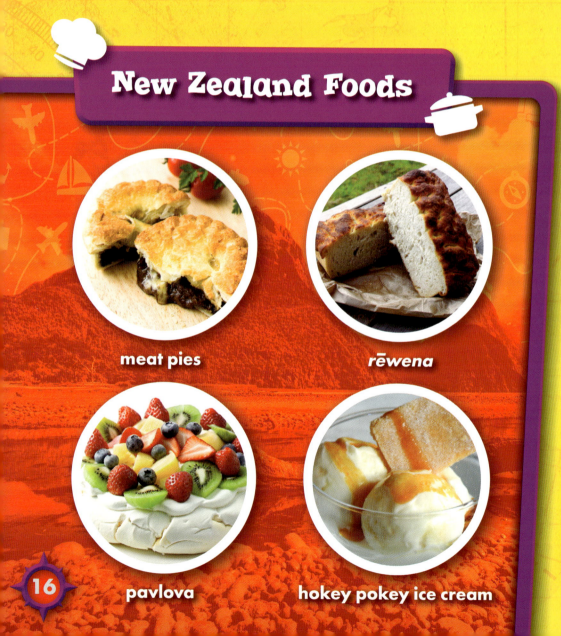

meat pies

rēwena

pavlova

hokey pokey ice cream

fish and chips

Pavlova is a fruity dessert. Hokey pokey ice cream is made with **toffee**!

February 6 is Waitangi Day. People enjoy concerts and parades.

Matariki is the Māori New Year. People share food and play music. They honor Māori **culture**!

Matariki

Waitangi Day

New Zealand Facts

Size:
103,799 square miles
(268,838 square kilometers)

Population:
5,161,211 (2024)

National Holiday:
Waitangi Day (February 6)

Main Languages:
English, Māori

Capital City:
Wellington

Famous Face

Name: Peter Jackson

Famous For: director who made The Lord of the Rings and The Hobbit movie series

Religions

- other: 11%
- Hindu: 3%
- Christian: 37%
- none: 49%

Top Landmarks

Hobbiton Movie Set

Milford Sound

Te Puia

Glossary

background—a person's experiences, knowledge, and family history

bungee jump—to jump from a high place while attached to a long, strong rope that stretches and stops you from hitting the ground

climate—the usual weather conditions of a place

culture—the beliefs, arts, and ways of life in a place or society

hot springs—places where warm water flows out of the ground

Indigenous—related to people originally from an area

insects—small animals with six legs and bodies divided into three parts

toffee—a type of candy made by boiling sugar and butter together

traditional—related to customs, ideas, or beliefs handed down from one generation to the next

volcanoes—holes in the earth; when a volcano erupts, hot ash, gas, and melted rock called lava shoot out.

To Learn More

AT THE LIBRARY

Furze, Katie. *Tuatara: A Living Treasure*. Auckland, N.Z.: Scholastic NZ, 2023.

Mather, Charis. *A Visit to New Zealand*. Minneapolis, Minn.: Bearport Publishing, 2023.

Spanier, Kristine. *New Zealand*. Minneapolis, Minn.: Jump!, 2022.

ON THE WEB

FACTSURFER

Factsurfer.com gives you a safe, fun way to find more information.

1. Go to www.factsurfer.com.
2. Enter "New Zealand" into the search box and click 🔍.
3. Select your book cover to see a list of related content.

Index

animals, 5, 10, 11
Aoraki, 7
arts, 14
Auckland, 12
bungee jump, 15
capital (see Wellington)
climate, 8
English, 12
food, 16, 17, 18
forests, 10
hike, 15
hot springs, 6
Māori, 12, 13, 14, 16, 18
map, 5
Matariki, 18
mountains, 6, 7, 9, 10, 15
New Zealand facts, 20-21
North Island, 6
people, 5, 12, 14, 15, 18
rain, 9
rugby, 15

say hello, 13
ski, 15
snow, 9
South Island, 6, 9, 11
South Pacific Ocean, 4
volcanoes, 6
Waitangi Day, 18, 19
Wellington, 4, 5

The images in this book are reproduced through the courtesy of: Poeyy, front cover; CWresh, p. 3; Robert CHG, pp. 4-5; NuFa Studio, p. 5; donvictorio, p. 6; Taras Vyshnya, pp. 6-7; Dmitry Pichugin, pp. 8-9, 21 (Milford Sound); 1lg1n, p. 9; ChameleonsEye, pp. 10-11; Jiri Prochazka, p. 11 (North Island brown kiwi); trabantos, p. 11 (tuatara); Mark, p. 11 (Hector's dolphin); Christopher Stephens/ Wikipedia, p. 11 (Cook strait giant wētā); Stargrass, p. 12; kaz_c, pp. 12-13; Michael Williams/ Alamy Stock Photo, pp. 14-15; Photoimagesnz, p. 15 (skiing); Henrique Daniel Araujo, p. 15 (bungee jumping); NaturalBox, p. 16 (meat pies); eqroy, p. 16 (rēwena); Maria Alam Sraboni, p. 16 (pavlova); Ben Sutherland/ Wikipedia, p. 16 (hokey pokey ice cream); LazingBee, p. 17; Lynn Grieveson/ Getty Images, p. 18; NataliaCatalina, pp. 18-19; Hybrid Gfx, p. 20 (flag); LFP/ Alamy Stock Photo, p. 20 (Peter Jackson); Summit Art Creations, p. 21 (Hobbiton Movie Set); kdreams, p. 21 (Te Puia); Eric Isselee, p. 23.